D1410783

GETTING PAID TO
Produce
Videos

CAROL HAND

ROSEN
PUBLISHING®

New York

Published in 2017 by The Rosen Publishing Group, Inc.
29 East 21st Street, New York, NY 10010

Copyright © 2017 by The Rosen Publishing Group, Inc.

First Edition   MAY 0 8 2017

Library of Congress Cataloging-in-Publication Data

Names: Hand, Carol, 1945– author.
Title: Getting paid to produce videos / Carol Hand.
Description: First edition. | New York : Rosen Publishing, 2017. | Series:
 Turning your tech hobbies into a career | Includes bibliographical references
 and index.
Identifiers: LCCN 2016023771 | ISBN 9781508172925 (library bound)
Subjects: LCSH: Video recordings—Production and direction—Vocational
 guidance—Juvenile literature. | Internet videos—Production and
 direction—Vocational guidance—Juvenile literature. | Mass
 media—Vocational guidance—Juvenile literature. | CYAC: Vocational
 guidance.
Classification: LCC TK5105.8867 .H36 2017 | DDC 384.558—dc23
LC record available at https://lccn.loc.gov/2016023771

Manufactured in Malaysia

Contents

Introduction

While many people make YouTube videos that are funny, informative, or socially relevant, few actually become rich and famous doing so. One who did is known by the username PewDiePie.

PewDiePie was born Felix Arvid Ulf Kjellberg in Gothenburg, Sweden, on October 24, 1989. PewDiePie, then just Felix, graduated from a private high school in his hometown and entered Chalmers University of Technology, headed for a degree in industrial economics and technology management. But in 2010, he decided a YouTube career sounded like more fun, and he left college. "Dropping the news to my parents that I was skipping my 'dream education' at Chalmers to sit at home recording videos while playing video games was not easy," he says. To pay the bills while he got started, Felix took a job at a hot dog stand. Two years later, he had more than one million YouTube viewers, and he is still setting records.

By early 2016, he had the most YouTube subscribers (forty-two million) and the most views (more than eleven billion) in the world. In subscription numbers, PewDiePie has eclipsed competitors such as One Direction (nineteen million), Justin Bieber (eighteen million), and Rihanna (eighteen million). He has produced about 2,600 videos. PewDiePie's wealth varies according to who is describing it. The website Celebrity Net Worth says he has $12 million. Money Nation lists his net worth

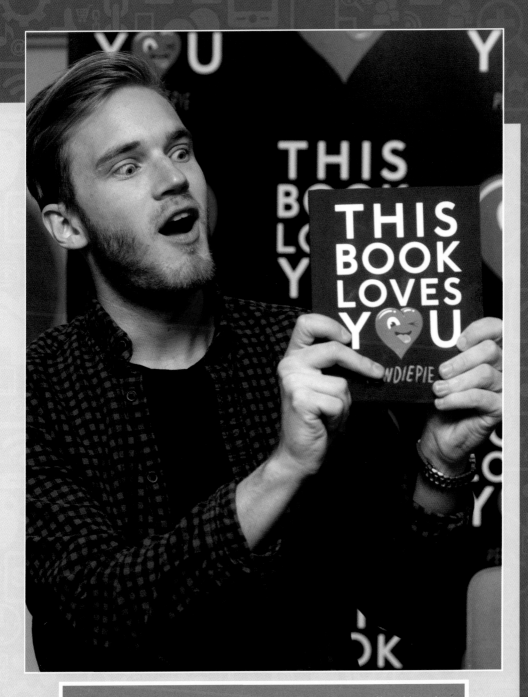

PewDiePie is branching out from YouTube as an author. Here, he launches his new book, titled *This Book Loves You*, on October 18, 2015, during a photo call at Waterstones Piccadilly, London.

at $61 million. They based this high value on estimates of his YouTube channel earnings along with investments, minus taxes and expenses.

Whatever it is now, PewDiePie's wealth is likely to grow. In 2016, he launched his own entertainment network, Revelmode. He is partnering with Maker Studios, which is owned by Disney. He describes the venture as "me and a group of YouTubers coming together to do awesome things." It will feature game and video development, community events, charity programs, and original video content by PewDiePie and his "group" (which includes other YouTube stars such as CinnamonToastKen, CutiePieMarzia, EmmaBlackery, and Jelly).

How did a Swedish schoolboy develop a YouTube empire? As he describes it, "I make funny videos of me playing video games, and I share those moments." PewDiePie's success has a lot to do with his unique style and personality. His videos have been described as outlandish and include shouting and screaming, funny or tongue-in-cheek remarks, and profanity. They also boost the sales of the video games he plays. About his goals, he has said "I just want to entertain," and "I'm not out to max my income." He refers to his fans as "bros" and his subscribers as the "Bro Army." With their help, PewDiePie has also become active in charity work. He has raised more than $1 million for charities including World Wildlife Fund, St. Jude's Hospital, Charity: Water, and Save the Children.

PewDiePie is one-half of a "YouTube power couple." In 2011, he met fashion and makeup vlogger Marzia Bizognin when she emailed to tell him she found his videos funny. They have collaborated on several projects, including a miniseries promoting the horror movie *As Above, So Below*. Bizognin's own YouTube channel, CutiePieMarzia, has more than six million subscribers and has earned more than 470 million views.

Chapter ONE

What Is Video Production?

A career in video production can be many things, from producing short online videos to producing full-scale Hollywood movies or television shows. People take many routes to become producers. Some begin, as PewDiePie did, by building on a hobby. He began making YouTube videos on a topic he loved. Others begin as writers, photographers, or film buffs and go to college to obtain degrees in film production. Regardless of the path taken, video production can be an exciting, rewarding career for the right person. Having a related hobby makes it that much easier to get started.

Going to the movies is a pleasurable and memorable experience shared by couples and friends. Thus, the potential video producer has the opportunity to make many people happy.

WHAT DOES A VIDEO PRODUCER DO?

Any successful maker of YouTube videos has already been a writer, director, camera operator, editor, and producer—not to mention promoter, business manager, and probably several other job titles. How hard can it be to "just" produce a video? It should be a lot less work than doing everything yourself, right?

Not really. As projects become bigger and more expensive, participants' responsibilities become more specialized—and usually more difficult. Different people do each job, and the producer rules them all. The producer is the top executive, or decision maker, on any movie, television show, or online video production. Producers manage video projects. They make all major decisions related to funding, budget, staffing, scheduling, and troubleshooting. They make or approve changes to script, crew, or cast during the production process. Producers shape the project. They act as both creators and entrepreneurs.

Because the producer's job encompasses the entire project, it includes hundreds of specific tasks. One task is finding a script. This might include selecting an idea (the producer's own idea, an already existing script, or a play or book), writing or cowriting and editing the script, or locating a scriptwriter to write it. Another is arranging financing for the project. This requires locating and negotiating with people who have the funds to complete the project—and keeping them happy by not going over budget during production! The producer conducts meetings with staff. This allows face-to-face communication with high-level personnel (such as directors, screenwriters, and department managers) to keep the project on schedule and within budget. Meetings also allow personnel to coordinate activities across departments. The producer monitors postproduction activities to ensure that all details of the project are completed.

These duties are performed by well-established producers in Hollywood, New York, and other large-scale production venues. But before a producer can tackle projects at that level, he or she has probably had years of experience at lower levels in the video production industry.

BUILDING GOOD VIDEO SKILLS

One of the easiest ways to get started in video production is to learn to use your smartphone or handheld video camera to make videos. Your first goal should not be making money, but building skills so you can make good videos that people will pay to see. Regardless of the topic, good videos look professional. VTREP, an online magazine for video entrepreneurs, lists seven factors essential for professional-looking videos: good lighting; good audio; holding the phone or camera steady; getting close to the subject; holding the phone horizontally rather than vertically so the video will look good on any screen; using mobile apps that add professional features; and being prepared by having all gear, props, scripts, and actors present before beginning a shoot.

Many business professionals now advertise online. They produce short (often fifteen-second) videos on YouTube, Vimeo, or Viddy. Their goal is to give their companies a "face," instead of showing only products and services. To improve the quality of such videos, Tim Parker of Intuit suggests the following: use high-quality equipment for shooting and editing; avoid "cool" effects—they take too long to load and the audience won't wait; use a simple background and a lot of light; keep editing simple;

compress videos; and keep videos short, splitting them up if necessary (four minutes is the absolute maximum). These pointers apply to anyone who wants to make outstanding online videos.

Editing is the "postproduction" aspect of video production. After the video has been shot, it must be cut and assembled, and audio and special effects (if any) added. Expert editing can turn a good video into a great one. This requires video editing software. Examples of software packages accessible to the beginning video producer include WeVideo, Magisto, YouTube Video Editor, Video Toolbox, and FileLab. Before choosing a video editor, video producers should carefully compare features and decide which ones they cannot live without.

A business seeking to advertise online needs a video producer who understands the video-making process and equipment.

MAKING MONEY BY MAKING VIDEOS

The ways to make money with videos are limited only by the imagination. VTREP lists several venues needing videos that young, enthusiastic video producers can supply. Some are available in the video maker's hometown and school. These include weddings, anniversaries, funerals or memorials, birthday parties, and school events (such as basketball games and other competitions and cheerleading). Young producers might make videos of local musicians and bands, real estate open houses, or local businesses. They might shoot video résumés for people applying for jobs or college.

Many—perhaps most—video producers start on YouTube. This website, which is owned by Google, allows registered users to upload videos so they can be viewed, shared, and commented upon. People serious about making money on YouTube set up their own YouTube channel—a home page where they list their videos and information about themselves. Then, they figure out the best ways to monetize, or make money from the site. At first, people ran ads with videos or sold their own products using "in-video advertisements," that is, briefly mentioning the product in the video. These methods are still used, but newer YouTubers are experimenting with more creative monetizing methods. Some people partner with larger companies that specialize in distribution and take over marketing of the products. Others are turning their fans into patrons, who support production of a video by donating on sites such as Kickstarter or Indiegogo. There are also sites, such as Patreon, where fans can make general donations to YouTube stars they like, rather than donating for a specific project.

Regardless of the monetizing method, the video producer must develop a large following to make money on YouTube. Part of this is luck, part is good marketing, and part is making professional-looking videos. Another important part is producing a video (or series of videos) with content that people really want to see. As your following grows, you can get more and better advertisers. Producing a single hit can do it, as the South Korean singer Psy did with his hit "Gangnam Style." A series of videos

South Korean rapper Psy performs in New York City, on May 3, 2013. His viral video hit "Gangnam Style" brought K-Pop (Korean Pop) back onto the international scene.

on the same subject also works; for example, the comedy team Smosh (www.smosh.com) is one of YouTube's most popular channels.

If YouTubers make videos with a unique style or sought-after educational content, they can become celebrities, and money comes to them. In addition to online advertising, people may seek them out for paid appearances and speaking engagements. One example is Laci Green, who runs a popular sex education channel called Sex+. Green now does speaking engagements at schools and other sites attracting young people.

WHY BE A VIDEO PRODUCER?

There are probably as many reasons for becoming a YouTube video producer as there are people aspiring to the career. Some people simply love making videos. Some want to become rich and famous; others want to make some extra money. Still others just want to interact with people who share their interests, whether video games, humor, movies, or cute puppies. Another group is not interested in making money for themselves, but instead, wants to promote and raise money for good causes. Many do this by enrolling in the YouTube Nonprofit Program.

The amount of money a YouTube entrepreneur can make is impossible to pinpoint. It varies widely depending on the number of subscribers and site visits, the type and amount of advertising on the site, and, of course, the content. Only a few become multimillionaires. Those with content that interests millions of people (for example, video games or sports) will get more visits and make more money than those with very specialized interests. One of the latter is Scott Driscoll, an engineer who has made videos on topics such as electronics soldering, headphone

Making Videos with Drones

The word "drone" usually conjures images of unmanned aerial vehicles (UAVs) with remotely located operators dropping bombs in faraway war zones. But smaller civilian drones are now serving more peaceful purposes, such as search and rescue; monitoring hurricanes; and inspecting bridges, dams, and pipelines. They are also expected to become important in law enforcement, although privacy concerns make this use highly controversial.

The technology needed to use drones in video projects is already available. Remote-controlled model airplanes and helicopters (unmanned aircraft systems, or UAS) are relatively inexpensive and easy to use. Cameras have become smaller and lighter and have higher resolutions and better lenses. Most importantly, they can be fitted with gimbals, instruments that stabilize them during flight.

A person with a drone-mounted camera can make money in many ways. The YouTube Channel Team BlackSheep posts stunning videos from a drone's perspective. They show daredevil stunts and aerial views from around the globe. With some experience, video producers can use small drones in professional situations, from news coverage to security to advertising. The beginning drone videographer would probably start with

(continued on the next page)

(continued from the previous page)

simpler jobs, such as shooting outdoor weddings or sporting events.

However, caution is required. Many people are annoyed, or even threatened, by drones buzzing overhead. Drone users must consider safety issues, such as potential collisions with bystanders or other aircraft. They must follow Federal Aviation Administration (FAA) regulations for model aircraft. Users do not need FAA permission to fly drones for recreation. But FAA authorization is required if they use the drone to make a for-profit video.

wrapping, and Bitcoin. Driscoll says, "At least for my videos, a minimum wage job would have been a higher paid use of my time." During a six-year period (2007 to 2013), his videos had more than four million views and made a total of $5,675.51, or $1.62 per thousand views. In the last month of his tally (September 2013), he made $264, or about $3.67 per thousand views. Driscoll hopes that continued viewing of his videos will eventually pay off.

"Traditional" video producers might work in television or movie studios or in the marketing department of a business. Some of these producers work for themselves. Others receive a salary, which varies according to the location and importance of the position to the organization. Anyone interested in how much money a traditional video producer makes can get an idea by consulting the Occupational Outlook Handbook on the Bureau of Labor Statistics website. This site describes each occupation

Claudia Sulewski began her career with the YouTube channel BeyondBeautyStar. In 2015, she became Teen Vogue's official YouTube host, and she is now moving into acting.

and gives a salary range, which is updated annually. According to the OOH, the job outlook for producers and directors is high through 2024, but competition for these jobs is intense. Aspiring producers are more competitive if they have good business skills.

Video production is a highly varied field and anyone with a smartphone can participate. But making it a career is not always easy. Except for the lucky person with a unique talent, interest, or personality, video production will not lead to instant (or even near-instant) riches. It will require a thorough knowledge of the type of production career you want along with hard work and dedication to move forward in that career.

Chapter TWO

Getting Your Video Education

A good video producer is highly educated. This does not necessarily mean having many degrees (or even one). It does mean knowing a great deal about a great many things. Video production involves art, science, technology, and business—at the very least. The educational path taken by each video producer is unique. It depends on the person's interests—do you want to produce short YouTube videos or advertising videos for businesses? Do you want to make

Producer Morgan Spurlock talks with a cast member during the filming of his 2008 documentary, *Where in the World Is Osama Bin Laden?*

music or instructional videos? Or is your ultimate goal to produce long films for Hollywood—movies, television shows, or documentaries? Whatever type of videos you choose, much of the education needed will be similar. Video producers must know, and ideally be able to perform in some capacity, the job of every person on the production set. They must learn how to act, direct, operate a camera, and edit. They need business management, promotion, and leadership skills. They must communicate with many different kinds of people.

TURN YOUR HOBBY INTO A CAREER

While there is no single "correct" path to a video production career, the person who makes videos as a hobby has a big head start because he or she is already a video producer on a small scale. Practicing this hobby will help you learn the basics. Some successful video producers combine two hobbies. PewDiePie is one example. Warren Miller is another. Miller has created more than 750 films. His video production company, Warren Miller Entertainment, is the world's foremost maker of skiing and snowboarding movies.

The more time you spend watching videos online at sites such as YouTube, Vimeo, and Dailymotion, the more information you will soak up about how videos are made. Learning to watch online videos critically can help you learn the difference between good and bad videos. The same is true for the person who wants to make Hollywood films. Just ask filmmaker Quentin Tarantino, whose movies include *Pulp Fiction, Django Unchained,* and *Jackie Brown*. Tarantino's first job was clerking in a video store, where he discussed films and made recommendations to

Warren Miller has made a career with snowboarding and skiing movies. Action is essential for most good videos, such as this shot of a snowboarder in the Swiss Alps.

customers. Of his education, he says, "When people ask me if I went to film school I tell them, 'No, I went to films.'"

HIGH SCHOOL AND ONLINE COURSES

Anyone serious about a career in video production can begin in high school. According to the College Board, helpful high school courses for aspiring video producers include art, theater arts, photography, computer/graphic arts, computer applications, AP art history, and AP English literature courses. These courses provide the basics of many necessary skills, as well as background in the intellectual basis of filmmaking. Why is the intellectual basis important? Any good video is mainly good because of its content. Filmmaker Anthony Q. Artis says, "…work on creating videos—any kind of videos—that impact people, that move them, that excite them, that make them laugh, cry, ponder the ideas you've presented them with—any kind of videos that tell a story." The more stories you read in literature and watch in films, the more depth and quality your own video stories will have.

Those wanting a head start on a film career can also tap into the many excellent online courses, some free or low cost. For example, Production 101 is a complete online course for beginners; it covers editing, shooting, sound, lighting, lenses, and video technology. Individuals can complete it, but it is also used by many schools. Reel Marketer lists its pick of the top fifteen video courses available online. Several of these involve use of editing software. A number of universities have free online college-level film courses and materials. A Google search using the keywords "video production online courses" will yield many tutorials and training courses. Aspiring video producers should definitely check these out.

COLLEGE DEGREES

Most (although not all) people who excel in the field of film production have a fine arts degree from an accredited college. There are three basic degrees: associate of fine arts, or AFA (a two-year degree); bachelor of fine arts, or BFA (a four-year degree); and a graduate degree, master of fine arts or MFA, which is obtained after the BFA. For most people, the typical degree is the BFA, and the most obvious major is film production, or a similar major such as cinema and television production.

Videos are essential in the field of education, as online learning expands. The internet is bringing education to people around the world, and video producers can be leaders in this revolution.

Students following this path learn to make movies. They also study movies to learn how they are put together and what makes them good or bad. They take courses in subjects such as animation, cinematography and videography, digital editing, directing, screenwriting, sound design and production, and studio television production.

A film production major includes considerable hands-on experience. Students both make their own movies and work on movies made by their classmates. As student producers, they spend many hours assembling a cast, crew, and props (sometimes spending their own money on props); shoot and edit scenes multiple times; and take criticism from both professors and classmates. They are expected to follow orders while working on their classmates' projects. During class projects, they serve in many roles—working with video and sound equipment, editing, or acting as production managers (coordinating equipment, schedules, space, and actors). These varied experiences will help the student, after graduation, feel at home on a professional film set. Film production is a high-pressure major. Students must be creative, hardworking, and patient. But in the end, they will see their own complex video projects on the big screen.

Sometimes only professors and fellow students see the work done in college video production classes. But, for the Hollywood bound, it's good to know that student filmmakers sometimes win Oscars. Some Student Academy Award winners have become highly successful. These include John Lasseter (*Toy Story*), Trey Parker (*South Park*), Robert Zemeckis (*Back to the Future*), and Spike Lee, a prolific producer, director, and actor who owns the production company 40 Acres and a Mule Filmworks. Like Lee, most famous producers wear many hats during their careers.

At various times, they work not only as producers, but also as screenwriters, directors, animators, and actors.

OTHER COURSES AND MAJORS

Film production majors also include business courses that teach aspiring producers (among other things) how to set up and run a production, who does what on a set, how a script is sold, and how to finance and distribute a film. In 2016, for example, the USC School of Cinematic Arts offered courses including Breaking into the Film Industry, Insiders: The Art & Commerce of Hollywood, and Outsiders: Independent Feature Filmmaking and Distribution. BFA candidates at Columbia College Hollywood can choose an emphasis on producing. This includes business-related courses such as Hollywood Business Practices & History, Entertainment Law, Art of the Pitch, and Marketing & Public Relations.

Other majors related to video production can also provide entrance into the field. These include animation and special effects, broadcast journalism, film studies, photography, design and visual communication, and theater design and stagecraft. A student might major in one of these fields and transition into video production later in their career. If a specific part of the moviemaking process really excites you, that is likely the major you should choose.

CHOOSING THE RIGHT COLLEGE

Courses and degree programs in film production are available throughout the United States. Where you go depends on several things. First, what is the content of the curriculum? Does it provide the courses and type of training you want? Second, what is the cost? Can you afford it, or will it saddle you with years of debt? Third, is the location close to home and therefore more affordable? Or is it farther away, but worth the move because it is a location where you want to live and work?

An online search for universities with film production degrees provides a long list of choices. The website Best Colleges gave this list of the ten best film school choices in 2015: Vanderbilt University, University of Chicago, University of Southern California, New York University, Cornell University, Columbia

The Savannah College of Art and Design has campuses in Atlanta, Georgia; Hong Kong; and Lacoste, France. The school has more than 10,000 students. The Atlanta campus is shown here.

University, University of California–Berkeley, University of Pennsylvania, Yale University, and University of California–Los Angeles.

The *Hollywood Reporter* makes a yearly list of the top twenty-five film schools. Not surprisingly, they include all of the schools in the top ten list above. Other notable schools on their 2015 list include California Institute of the Arts, Chapman University, Loyola Marymount University, Wesleyan University, University of Texas–Austin, Boston University, Stanford University, University of North Carolina School of the Arts, and Savannah College of Art and Design. Many colleges not listed also have excellent programs. Prospective students should first decide what they want in a major and what location they prefer. Then, a thorough online search can help determine which colleges meet their needs.

Beware of For-Profit Universities!

An important consideration is whether a university is for profit or nonprofit. All college degrees are expensive, but for-profit universities are extremely expensive. Two well-known for-profit universities in the area of media arts are Full Sail University, based in Winter Park, Florida, and the Art Institutes, which have a system of more than fifty

(continued on the next page)

(continued from the previous page)

campuses around the country. For-profit universities look wonderful on paper and online. They offer many courses, professional staff working in the industry, and ties with major companies to help graduates get jobs.

But students have many criticisms of for-profit programs. Students enrolled at various Art Institute campuses say that the programs taught out-of-date methods, hired too few teachers, and provided weak career advice. Others stated that there appeared to be no standards for admission. Also, credits earned could not be transferred to other schools, leaving students feeling trapped. According to Ben Miller, senior director for postsecondary education at the Center for American Progress, these colleges have a "very sophisticated marketing machine… They prey on people's insecurities about their self worth."

Although traditional state or private (nonprofit) colleges or universities are expensive, too, they are much less expensive. Nonprofit universities usually have a century or more of experience and tradition, making them stable and trustworthy. They provide help obtaining scholarships, fellowships, grants, or (as a last resort) loans to pay college expenses. They also have respected faculty and strong programs for launching graduates into their new careers.

SCHOLARSHIPS AND FUNDING SOURCES

For many people, the deciding factor in choosing a college or university is cost. Scholarships can help with this. The first place to look for college scholarships is in your own high school and community, where people know you and there is less competition. The organization Scholarship America cautions that most film-related scholarships are earmarked for students already in college. They suggest that high school students focus on other achievements that might earn scholarships for the first year of college. But if you made videos during your high school years, by all means use them. Enter the best ones in contests. Put together a digital portfolio, including only your best work,

Choosing a college, applying for admission, and applying for scholarships and grants takes time and commitment.

and use it as part of your application both for college and for scholarships and fellowships.

Many universities have general scholarships, fellowships, or grants available to all entering freshmen, including those in film production and related fields. A great variety of funding sources are available. There are general scholarships for students of filmmaking, specific ones (for example, for women in media), and grants for student production or research proposals. Online sites provide lists of available scholarships for students in media. These include Scholarship.com, Scholarship America, and the Kodak Student Scholarship Program. Universities have their own specific scholarships and grants. Serious students should apply for scholarships throughout their college careers. Scholarships probably will not pay your entire college costs, but they will help. They will also show that you excel in your chosen field, which will help in your post-graduate job search.

Deciding the type of program and college that works best for you is a very personal decision. But video production is a public career. As a producer, you put your creations—your "babies"— out into the world, where they can be analyzed and perhaps destroyed by viewers and critics. Whether you choose college or another educational path into video production, you are choosing to make yourself a public figure. Consider this choice carefully, and be sure you understand what it means.

Chapter THREE

Skills Needed to Make Videos

T he internet appears wide open for aspiring video producers. Those producing their own videos must first have a talent or idea that people will pay to see or that advertisers will sponsor. A producer who is also the star must have an on-screen presence—charisma that will make people want to watch. Passion for your topic and a desire to share it must shine through. But, whether you sit in your living room producing YouTube videos, make two-minute advertising videos for businesses, or strive to become the next top Hollywood producer, you

For many aspiring video producers, YouTube represents the beginning of an exciting career. The video-sharing website was created by three former PayPal employees.

will require a skill set that is both broad and deep. This includes personal, technical, and business-related skills. Greater skill will translate to greater success.

PERSONAL SKILLS

Some of a producer's most important personal skills include self-confidence, leadership skills, and strong communication skills. Middle- or high-school students might practice for a future career by writing and producing their own short movies, with friends as cast and crew. The authors of the book *Filmmaking for Teens* describe some of the skills needed to produce these first films:

> "This job will challenge your organizational and social skills, but it can also be a great deal of fun. You'll master the fine art of asking favors, mooching, solving problems, begging, working out differences of opinion, and getting things at a discount. You'll be the leader of a band of crazy filmmakers."

As you graduate to producing larger-scale videos, all of these skills will come in handy. Before the project begins, a producer must present, or pitch, a movie concept to potential financial backers and persuade them to fund it. Pitching requires good speaking skills, the ability to describe a concept concisely, the ability to negotiate and compromise—and, of course, self-confidence. Once the project starts, producers must be able to work well with the director, crew, and cast. They must keep the project running smoothly and efficiently. They must be self-motivated, and they must be able to motivate others, even under pressure.

A good producer is highly creative, a critical thinker, and an expert problem solver. He or she must have a creative vision—a clear mental picture of the final product—and be able to guide the cast and crew to make this vision a reality. To do this, a producer must be able to organize. This means managing time and resources, including people. Producers organize the entire video project—from hiring to delegating responsibility within each department to setting and maintaining rehearsal and shooting schedules. This means being highly flexible. It means being able to switch jobs quickly and being prepared for long, irregular hours and frequent travel. In a complex project such as a movie, many jobs must be done simultaneously. This means the producer must multitask, or juggle many responsibilities.

BUSINESS SKILLS

If you make one-person videos for YouTube (with you as screenwriter, actor, director, and producer), you will likely monetize your videos as described in chapter one: by selling ads, partnering with distribution companies, or finding patrons. You can add to your business skills by making short films with your friends (for example, finding free or discount props). All of these skills will help as you advance to the production of larger-scale films, videos, or television shows. They will just need to be expanded to match the larger scale and budget of your new projects.

A producer needs superb negotiation skills to obtain funding for a film project. Negotiation is a business as well as a personal skill. To negotiate well, the producer must determine how much money will be needed for the project and understand which areas can be trimmed and which cannot. Once the project is funded, the producer handles the budget. This requires a good head for business, including strong mathematical abilities and a background in math and accounting. Producers must consider the budget throughout the production process. In preproduction, they must approve locations, hire studio personnel, accept a

Overcoming Race and Gender Obstacles

For women and ethnic minorities, a special skill for making it in Hollywood is the toughness and perseverance to succeed in spite of many obstacles. In the past few years, successful producers in the minority community have become more visible. Television producer Shonda Rhimes is one such success. Rhimes was honored as a game changer in 2014, in the special Women of Power issue of *Black Enterprise*.

In 2016, Rhimes, an ABC executive producer, had three hit television drama series (*Grey's Anatomy, Scandal,* and *How to Get Away with Murder*) and premiered a fourth series, *The Catch*. She was the network's top drama earner. When Rhimes received a Diversity Award from the Directors Guild of America, she spoke of her frustration with Hollywood's hiring practices. "There's such a lack of people hiring women and minorities that when someone does it on a regular basis, they are given an award," she said. "It's not because of a lack of talent. It's because of a lack of access. People hire who they know. If it's been a white boys club for 70 years, that's a lot of white boys hiring one another."

Mara Brock Akil, a producer for the BET (Black Entertainment Television) Network, was also honored in the 2014 issue of *Black Enterprise*. Akil has produced *The Game*, the Grammy-nominated series *Girlfriends*, and the

Shonda Rhimes and actress Kerry Washington attend the White House Correspondents' Dinner on April 27, 2013. Rhimes has been a game changer in hiring women and minorities.

hit series *Being Mary Jane*. Akil says, "Diversity is a business, and we're hoping to fill that void of shortsightedness."

Minority movie producers, both male and female, are also achieving increased recognition. They include Effie Brown, Debra Martin Chase, Ava DuVernay, Nelson George, and the team of Rob Hardy and Will Packer.

final script, and develop a production schedule and budget. Doing all of these parts carefully can save money later. During production, staying on schedule means staying on budget. After production and postproduction (during which the video is edited and assembled) comes marketing and distribution. To plan how to get the video out to the public, the producer must work with finance and distribution companies. Again, this requires understanding budgets.

Safety is also key in the film or video production business, especially during the production stage. Producers must

Here, a film crew works to produce a video clip. No matter how small or large the production is, a video producer must always follow all safety rules on set.

understand all laws and procedures required to maintain a safe workplace. The studio must be set up to prevent cast and crew injuries. The producer must make sure that all safety laws and regulations are strictly followed.

Only rarely does a producer show equal talent at all stages of production—obtaining funding, preproduction, production, and postproduction. But excellent producers strive to achieve competence in all areas. Being skilled at working within a strict budget and on a strict timeline are crucial to a producer's success.

EQUIPMENT FOR BEGINNERS

Producers must learn to use (or at least understand) the basic equipment required for all aspects of video making. For the beginning producer—say, a teen making his or her first videos—a simple way to get started is to set up a YouTube channel for video blogging, or vlogging. This means knowing how to use basic video and audio equipment. The producer should learn the specifications for each piece of equipment, what it is used for, and how to use it. This basic knowledge comes with practice and provides an excellent starting point for a video production career.

Beginning vloggers can make excellent videos using cellphone cameras or handheld video cameras such as a GoPro. The GoPro is nearly indestructible and is especially good for travel and for filming sports and other active events. For those with more money, the best video quality is obtained with a DSLR (digital single-lens reflex) camera. These cameras produce near-professional quality video. Vlogging about gaming requires a capture card, which connects to the game console, television, and computer. It records the game as you play it, and you

Certain kinds of video production require an intrepid producer plus specialized equipment such as this underwater camera, which is being used to shoot a moray eel on a coral reef.

can record commentary over it. PC gamers can record using programs such as Fraps or DXtory.

In a vlog, message or content is often more important than video, so excellent audio is essential. A simple microphone, such as the Logitech ClearChat, is inexpensive and provides high-quality raw sound (sound without compression or filters). For the best-quality sound, the Blue Snowball is a highly sensitive condenser microphone. Adding a pop filter neutralizes "explosive" sounds (such as the letters *b, d,* and *p*) during recording.

A college major in video production or a related media field allows the student to study and use the basic equipment required for audio and video on location or on a soundstage and for editing after the video is shot. Committed students and professionals constantly improve their technical skills by practicing on their own.

TECHNICAL SKILLS AND EXPERIENCE

The college graduate with a degree in video production will need several years of experience before actually being hired as a producer. Graduates must work their way up the ladder. This means doing a variety of jobs, some of them low level and poorly paid. During this time, aspiring producers can build and hone their technical skills. They often begin as production runners, the entry-level (lowest) job on the production staff. Runners help out wherever they are needed on the set. They do routine office tasks, such as answering telephones, filing paperwork, or entering data. They arrange lunch dates or transportation, distribute call sheets, coordinate extras, or do whatever else is needed. Although this may sound boring, the runner eventually gets to see everything that happens on the set. A job as a runner is an excellent opportunity to learn the entire process. It is also a great way to make contacts that can help you move up in the field. In television, the runner is called a production coordinator or production assistant.

There is no direct route to becoming a producer. As graduates gain experience (and make contacts), they might find work in research, marketing, or scriptwriting. They might work as editors, camera operators, video technicians, or directors. The jobs obtained will depend on the person's interest and expertise, but producers are certainly expected to understand directing and editing. Each new job should build your skill set. With sufficient

After receiving a degree in video production, aspiring video producers might work as production runners, doing routine tasks such as answering telephones.

experience, you might become an assistant producer, working directly under the producer and doing whatever he or she needs. The more varied your job résumé, the more prepared you will be when a producer spot finally opens up—or when you decide to go for it and produce your very own indie film.

Finally, any skilled producer must keep up with advancing technology. Education is never done because the field is always changing. Sometimes learning occurs naturally. You receive a new piece of equipment and practice using it. If a new piece of technology is particularly complex, you might receive on-the-job training or take a short course. Producers must always read widely, stay alert, and keep up with changing trends.

In general, producers must know a little of everything. They must have personal, business, and technical skills and be able to use any combination of these skills at any time. The producer's job is stressful and requires concentration and commitment. It is also highly creative and highly rewarding.

Chapter FOUR

Diving into the Video Production Business

Aspiring young producers can go in one of two general directions as adults. They can make (or continue) their own business, making whatever types of videos or movies they choose. Or, they can obtain a traditional degree and seek a traditional video production job. Many people make several direction changes during their careers. A person might have a side business making and selling tutorials or music videos online but still attend college and obtain a degree. After college, he might start

Low budgets are the rule for many beginning and independent video producers. Here, a cameraman, a sound engineer, and the producer shoot video.

a freelance business or a production company. Another might work her way up within a company and eventually become a movie or television producer. At some point, she might break away to start her own indie (independent) production company.

STICKING WITH YOUTUBE

Few people can make a living placing videos on YouTube. Maya Black, writing for Chron.com, notes that competition is making it more difficult to get noticed on YouTube. Most videographers make tutorials to sell a product, advertise a talent or skill, or share a hobby. If they are serious about making money, they open an AdSense account, link it to their YouTube account, and build an audience by promoting their videos on social media sites.

YouTube is now positioning itself to compete with television. It has opened studios in Los Angeles, London, and Tokyo, and launched more than one hundred new content channels. In April 2012, YouTube began a revenue-sharing program to open moneymaking possibilities to all video creators, who receive about half the proceeds from any ad. During the program's first year, there was a 25 percent upsurge in videos uploaded. Unfortunately, advertisers' rates also dropped by one-third. According to Dave Morgan, founder of a TV ad-targeting firm, "most of what's on YouTube is not what advertisers want."

Before deciding to become a YouTube entrepreneur, young video producers should understand exactly why they make videos. Do you produce videos to sell a product or to promote another skill or hobby? If so, you might choose to stick with YouTube and work on increasing site traffic and building an audience. Or, are you a video producer because you love making videos or because you want to tell a great story? If you fit the latter description, it might be time to branch out from YouTube.

Interviewing is a skill that improves with practice, but several things are always important: Be pleasant, be prepared, show what you can do for the company, and always say thank you.

A TRADITIONAL PRODUCTION JOB

Zach Downs is responsible for hiring new production staff at 12 Stars Media. Downs looks for more than a good résumé. He says, "when I look through job applications, I want to find something that stands out, makes me stop and think, and looks amazing." He wants to see a short (but unique) video that tells him who you are. Be creative and show your personality. At an interview, ask questions that show your interest in the company, and after the interview, always follow up with a "thank you."

Many people assume a college degree will easily land them in their dream job. This is seldom true, especially in the video production business, where competition can be brutal. Graduates interviewed within two years after finishing college described many challenges. They were competing with applicants who had more experience. They lacked personal connections, who could point them toward possible employment. Employers preferred to hire freelance (self-employed) or short-term workers, rather than pay a full-time salary. Companies hired from within—that is, they promoted someone already in the company, rather than hire an unknown person. One recent graduate was hired by a company after completing an internship at the company. Several graduates found jobs in other fields and fit in freelance work whenever possible.

But even with this long list of challenges, most graduates remained upbeat. They counseled patience, hard work, and good communication with potential employers. One graduate stressed, "Good work gets noticed." He also urged job seekers to "fight for good internships that are willing to teach you the ropes and give you real experience," rather than settling for those where you do only office work and get coffee.

After landing that first job, how do you make sure it lasts? David Wappel of ECG Productions lists five tips that worked for him, from his first day on the job. First, "work to learn and learn to work." Remember that the job is giving you experience and knowledge. Pay attention to everything, and learn it. Second, ask questions, but don't impede the work. If you don't understand something, file away your question and ask later. Third, listen and remember. Wappel heard a producer say he preferred emails with bullet points, so he used bullet points in his next email. "I'm pretty much convinced that's the reason I was called in to work with him again," he says. Fourth, offer to carry gear whenever possible. This helps you learn every piece of equipment, what case it goes in, and how it is put together. Finally, be invaluable. Look for ways to help so your employers can't imagine life without you. Before you know it, you will be moving up the ladder.

FREELANCING IN VIDEO PRODUCTION

Many small video producers are freelancers. Freelancers work independently, for different clients at different times, rather than having a single employer. Freelancing has pros and cons. One great advantage is controlling your own work life. You do not go to the same job from nine to five every day. You never get bored, because every job is different. But freelancing can also be stressful and insecure. Because there is no steady paycheck, the freelancer has to hustle for clients to pay the bills. Some freelancers advertise locally and get jobs by word of mouth. Many advertise on sites such as Upwork or LinkedIn. They post their profiles online, and people needing videos bid for their services. Or they browse the site for available jobs and offer their services. Freelance video producers work closely with clients, helping them make decisions about light, motion, and other factors to ensure that the finished video meets the client's needs.

Freelance producer Hal Landen specializes in corporate videos. He gives four reasons why this works for him. The first is variety. Landen has produced videos on topics ranging from dock building to lipstick manufacturing. He has worked behind the scenes at Tiffany's, AT&T, and the Federal Drug Enforcement Agency, among others. Second, corporate videos pay well. Landen's fees per project range from $5,000 to $25,000 or more. After renting equipment and hiring assistants, he still

When they first start out, freelance video producers may be one-person operations. They do everything themselves, so they must become experts on all aspects of the process.

gets most of the money, and he usually does several projects at once. Third, much of his business comes from referrals and repeat customers because he satisfies customers the first time. Fourth, Landen gets satisfaction from exercising his creativity to produce good videos that help his clients. "And if you don't think corporate videos are creative, think again," he says. "Many of these corporate productions rival network TV commercials."

STARTING A VIDEO PRODUCTION BUSINESS

Starting a business is never easy or glamorous. A video production business is no exception. No matter how small the business is clients expect the same quality of videos they would get from a major Hollywood studio. Competition is intense, and the first few years are difficult. Many new businesses fail. Every entrepreneur must be able to survive and pay bills during the early years before the business becomes profitable. Every entrepreneur must be willing to risk financial insecurity—including losing start-up money borrowed from family, friends, other investors, and banks. Often, it is the entrepreneur's knowledge of business, rather than of video production, that determines the company's success or failure.

Aspiring business owners might be tempted to dive right in and start making videos. But preparation is vital. Carefully following a series of steps will lay the foundation for a solid business structure. The first step is research—read books and magazines about video production, study websites, talk with others in the business and learn the trends. Then, consult business experts including tax consultants, attorneys, and accountants. Learn about the nitty-gritty business details. Decide on a tax structure. This will determine legal and financial protections for your business. The three basic types of tax structures are sole proprietorship (you own the business by yourself, and take all the risks), partnership (you own the business with a partner), or corporation (ownership and risk are shared by a group of investors). You should thoroughly understand the pros and cons of each type before choosing one.

At this point, decide exactly what products or services the business will offer and the business location. Write up a business plan that includes a business structure, start-up budget, and marketing plan. Only now should you look for loans, investors, or other sources of funding. And only when funding is in place should you begin your video production business.

Why start your own video production business? Everyone's story is different. R. Bruce Perry of Intermix Design had worked ten years as a producer for another company when the company went bankrupt. He faced a choice—find another job or start his own production company. He chose the latter. Hisani P. DuBose, owner/producer of Seven Generations Media, LLP, is a screenwriter who got tired of waiting to be discovered. "Sending scripts to Hollywood companies was a waste of time because they wouldn't respond," DuBose said. So she took a digital video course and now produces her own films. Lindsay Campbell is a young web video producer. She first produced long-running video series for large media companies, including Wallstrip and MobLogic (both part of CBS Interactive) and YouTube Nation (Dreamworks). In 2013, she founded her own company, Long Future Media, which she describes as "a full-service digital studio that takes stories from inception through delivery." Her new business has produced videos for companies including Twitter, Social Leverage, Stocktwits, Conde Nast, and Astronauts Wanted.

Indie Producers: Small Budgets, Big Results

Many excellent movies are made for $1 million or less by independent, or "indie," production companies. Besides their small budgets, indie companies usually have a core crew of ten or fewer people. Sometimes several small companies team up on a single project. Indie producers tend to make quality the first priority when producing a movie, ahead of size of budget or expected profit. Their best efforts often appear at film festivals, such as Utah's Sundance Film Festival.

Gilbert Films is run by producers Gary Gilbert and Jordan Horowitz. Gilbert's first film was *Garden State*, which won many awards, including an Independent Spirit Award for Best First Feature. Gilbert and Horowitz, along with Daniela Lundberg, produced *The Kids Are Alright*, another award-winning film. In 2010, Lundberg and Dan Crown founded Red Crown Productions, described by the New York Film Academy as an "indie powerhouse." EFO Productions was founded in 1998 by Randall Emmett and George Furla. EFO has produced more than eighty films, many of which have starred actors Al Pacino or Robert DeNiro.

Richard Klubeck, Zach Braff, Gary Gilbert, and Pamela Abdy of the movie *Garden State* pose at the 20th IFP Independent Spirit Awards.

Many documentary films are also indie productions. The 2015 Tribeca Film Festival featured two of these: *Indian Point*, about a New York nuclear power plant, was produced by Motto Pictures, the production company of Julie Goldman. *Orion: The Man Who Would Be King* is about a Nashville singer hired to impersonate Elvis Presley. Jeanie Findlay both produced and directed *Orion*.

The video production business is not easy. Your first goal, when breaking into the industry, should be to decide exactly what you want to do. Do you want a job with an established company, or do you want to build your own company? Will you work freelance, or do you prefer a salary? Whatever your goals, hard work, persistence—and of course, excellent video production skills—should eventually lead to the job of your dreams.

Chapter FIVE

The Future of Video Production

Richard DePaso of Aardvark Video & Media Productions sums up what he sees as major trends in video production: "there will be more of it and there will be more producers, good and bad, amateur and professional…More and more video will be produced, distributed and viewed online." Most online videos will be produced by amateurs. Those who succeed as professionals will be thoroughly skilled in using the newest technology and equipment.

THE FUTURE OF VIDEO EQUIPMENT

The biggest change in video production has been the lower cost of video equipment, which puts it within range of nearly everyone. New cameras and software are relatively easy to use, allowing most people to master the technical skills quickly. Lower prices and decreased difficulty together make video production possible even for amateurs. The future of video production is also linked

to advances in the related fields of television, computers, and the Web.

Technology is trending toward much higher resolution for video production and viewing. Resolution refers to the clarity or sharpness of a video image. Higher resolution indicates greater sharpness. It is measured by the number of dots (pixels) on a video or television screen. A 720-by-480-pixel screen (defined as standard resolution, or SD) displays 720 dots on 480 lines, or about 345,000 pixels. Standard resolution was replaced by high definition (HD), with 1,920 × 1,080 pixels. HD was replaced by ultra-high definition (UHD, or 4K), with 3,840 × 2,160 pixels, or four times the HD pixel count. DePaso considers UHD "just the beginning of a trend." In 2014, only 1 percent of US homes had 4K television, but the percentage grew five to six times within the next year. By 2020, almost half of US households will have a 4K television.

Here, a visitor at the Panasonic Center showroom in Tokyo, Japan, tries a 2016-model Panasonic AG-DVX200 memory card camera recorder.

HD video will continue to be around for many years. But by 2016, some smartphones already had UHD video capability. Also in 2016, a German company released a set of high-performance lenses, called HDFX360. These small lenses clip onto a smartphone. They enable it to create professional-quality DSLR images and eliminate the need for a large, expensive DSLR camera. After shooting UHD footage, producers need software capable of editing it. Rather than buying an expensive editing program, many video producers now rent professional software programs such as Adobe Creative Cloud, further decreasing costs. Finally, computer hardware must be able to handle the extra data produced by UHD resolution. It may take a few years for computer processors to catch up with video capabilities.

John Foundas of Foundation Digital Media points to another trend, toward smaller cameras and larger screens. Smaller cameras are easier to carry and maneuver; videographers can get shots that were once difficult or impossible. Smaller cameras also speed up shooting without compromising quality. Now that UHD is available, people expect and demand higher-quality images. Larger screens on televisions, monitors, and mobile devices will better display these high-definition pictures. Finally, although Foundas does not give specifics, he also hopes for improvements in audio quality and in techniques for seamlessly synchronizing audio and video.

FUTURE USES OF VIDEO

A quick glance through YouTube and Facebook shows vast quantities of amateur video content. Some of this video content is personal, made to entertain or to record an event. Some is business related, to show products or train employees. Most individuals and many companies are not overly concerned with

Candace Payne, the "Chewbacca Mom," became an internet sensation after she livestreamed a video of herself laughing uncontrollably in her Chewbacca mask.

video quality and will not hire professionals to produce their videos. This trend is likely to increase, resulting in fewer video jobs in these areas.

But live video streaming is an exploding trend. In live streaming, video content is highly compressed and sent continuously over the internet. It is decompressed and viewed immediately upon arrival. The viewer sees it in real time (as it is sent), rather than waiting for the entire file to download. Not long ago, live video streaming was very expensive and required intensive hardware. But with new technology, events can be live streamed wirelessly over computers or smartphones. This opens up a whole new world of possibilities.

Professional applications of live streaming, including meetings, training sessions, seminars, conferences, and presentations, are becoming common. During conferencing, people view content and computer screens remotely, while talking directly with other participants. Live streaming of high school and university classes can replace commuting and bring education to remote locations. Often live streaming is combined with on-demand availability of classes, so students can access them at more convenient times. Recreational and cultural activities, such as sports and concerts, may also be live streamed. Live streaming instantly connects many thousands of people around the world.

Smart TVs, with internet connectivity, are already becoming part of everyday life. They have web browsers so they can be used as computers, as well as to use applications such as Netflix for content viewing. The trend suggests that, in the near future, you will receive your favorite television shows over the internet rather than over standard broadcast channels. Content for all of these trending technologies will be provided by tomorrow's video producers.

THE FUTURE FOR BUSINESS VIDEO PRODUCERS

Writing for One Market Media (OMM), Jimm Fox provides insight into the future of aspiring video producers. He points out that some trends work against new producers—the low price of equipment and software makes amateur video production easier, and the rise of online production introduces competition from around the world. On the up side, a producer can turn professional with a minimal investment in equipment. "Having expensive video equipment doesn't make you a good video producer any more than having an expensive pen makes you a good writer," Fox cautions.

There is an ever-increasing demand for business videos. By 2017, 69 percent of consumer internet traffic will be video based, and video-on-demand will have nearly tripled. Video-on-demand (VOD) systems allow users to watch videos when they choose, rather than at a specific time. As television and other mass-audience content gives way to mobile viewing on one's own schedule, business videos will target smaller and more specialized audiences. Producers will be asked to produce and deliver customized videos.

Business video producers will need to specialize. They might become experts in a certain business field—health care or real estate, for example. They might become experts on a certain type or style of video, such as the two-minute explainer video (2minuteexplainer.com) that helps people understand technology (or another product) before they buy it. Successful video producers must be able to tell a client how video can help solve a business problem. Also, there is a trend away from

The rise of mobile viewing on smartphones and other small devices is changing the future of video production

today's fake or staged videos toward "real reality," or video that is not staged or only slightly staged. Unstaged videos capture people's real reactions to products and services. The spread of smartphone cameras makes this much easier. According to Fox, "Winning with fake is going to get tougher and tougher."

However, not fake does not mean unplanned. A successful video begins in preproduction, before the video is shot. Every video should target a specific business goal. The message, concept, and style must be nailed down before shooting begins. Many businesses still see videos as standalone items, but in the near future they will be integrated into the rest of the marketing plan. This includes designing videos for better SEO (search engine optimization). SEO is a tool for making web pages, websites, or videos easier to find in a web search. The more keywords and tags a search engine (such as Google, Yahoo, or Bing) picks up from the video, the more "hits" it will get. The more people who see it, the more valuable it is as a marketing tool. Finally, a video producer must have a method for measuring the success of each video. There are online programs to help with this.

THE FUTURE FOR ENTERTAINMENT VIDEO PRODUCERS

Overall, there will be far fewer openings for video producers in the entertainment field than in business, but this field is expanding, too. People always crave entertainment in the form of movies, television, and documentary films. Production of these products is following the same trends shaping business videos. Web video is expanding to include full-length entertainment productions that compete with television series. Rob Millis, founder of Dynamo Media, describes web producers as the greatest innovators

Actors Nathan Fillion, Felicia Day, and Neil Patrick Harris share a panel discussion at the *Dr. Horrible's Sing-Along Blog* reunion in 2015.

in film and video. He says they are rapidly bridging the gap between offline and online media.

At first, people involved in web video—both producers and actors—were trying to get noticed so they could build careers in television or the movies. Now, however, web video is catching on, and web entertainment is a category of its own. After a 2007 to 2008 strike by the Writers Guild of America (WGA), many movie professionals began looking for ways to create programming outside the confines of Hollywood studios. Screenwriter/director/producer Joss Whedon, actor Neil Patrick Harris, and web personality Felicia Day combined their talents to produce a full web film production, *Dr. Horrible's Sing-Along Blog*. Other entertainers, such as Will Ferrell and Kevin Pollak, followed suit. Web production is rapid and inexpensive, and working

Steven Spielberg and George Lucas

Two experts on the future of the entertainment business are Hollywood icons Steven Spielberg and George Lucas. The two producer/directors discussed the future of entertainment on a panel at the USC School of Cinematic Arts in 2013. Both predicted radical changes. Because so many forms of media are now competing for attention, they expect traditional movie blockbusters to become rare. Spielberg predicts, "There's eventually going to be a big meltdown…" and several high-budget movies will fail spectacularly. The result, Lucas says, will be fewer but bigger theaters. Movies will remain in theaters for a year or more and a movie ticket will cost $50 to $150, much as Broadway shows today do. Both Spielberg and Lucas see smaller, more personal, more "quirky" content being developed for and distributed by streaming video on demand. Today's television and movie business will soon become internet television, Lucas predicts.

The two also discussed the future of video games. Now Spielberg says, players value violence and have little empathy for the characters. "The second you get the controller, something turns off in the heart, and it becomes a sport," he says. Lucas thinks some empathetic games will appear within the next five years, aimed mostly at women and girls. But Spielberg looks forward to a time when there are no controllers or screens, and players are completely immersed in a three-dimensional game universe. "We've got to put the player inside the experience," he says. "That's the future."

outside the major studies allows entertainers more creativity and freedom. They can also build an immediate fan base.

Today's up-and-coming video producers live in an exciting time. Technology is changing rapidly, as are the concepts of what entertainment is and how it is delivered. Choices seem almost unlimited, and new producers can go in almost any direction. They can choose to produce for the big screens of Hollywood or for tiny smartphone screens. They can choose the excitement of the entertainment industry, the moneymaking potential of business videos, or anything in between. But in all cases, tomorrow's producers will need to be highly skilled with current technology and adept at keeping up with fast-moving trends.

Glossary

DSLR (digital single-lens reflex) The type of camera used for modern video production; it has high-quality optics and uses a digital imaging sensor rather than film.

entrepreneur A person who starts, organizes, and operates his or her own business and takes the financial risks necessary to make the business successful.

freelance Self-employed; working independently for different clients at different times, rather than having a single employer and a single paycheck.

gimbal A mechanism consisting of a set of rings pivoted at right angles that supports an instrument (such as a compass or camera), keeping it horizontal and stable in a moving vessel or aircraft.

indie film (or independent film) A feature film, often low-budget, produced and distributed outside the major film studios; described by many as "making the film you want to make" as opposed to making what the major studios demand.

monetize To set up a website so that it generates profit for the owner; can be done in various ways, including advertising, selling products, or producing and selling tutorials.

pitch A short verbal presentation to movie or television executives or other potential backers, describing an idea for a movie or television show and designed to persuade them to fund the project; also used as a verb, for example, "he pitched his idea to the millionaire."

postproduction The parts of the production process from completion of video shooting to creating a final master copy; includes video and sound editing and adding music and titles.

preproduction The planning part of the production process, after receiving funding but before shooting begins; includes scripting, story boarding, hiring, finding locations, and developing schedules.

production The part of the process of film/video making during which the actual shooting or recording takes place.

production runner The lowest job on the production crew; involves running errands, doing office work, and being on call to help wherever needed on the set.

resolution The sharpness or clarity of a picture on a video screen; measured in pixels (640 by 480 pixels displays 640 dots per line on 480 lines, for about 300,000 pixels).

SEO (search engine optimization) A tool for making websites, web pages, or videos easier for a search engine to find; involves use of keywords that increase the number of people clicking on the item.

streaming video Video content that is compressed and sent continuously (streaming) over the web, in real time; that is, it is decompressed as it arrives, and the viewer sees it without having to wait for it to download.

UHD (ultra high definition) Video resolution with very high pixel count (3,840 × 2,160 pixels), replacing high definition (HD, 1,920 x 1,080 pixels) and becoming standard by about 2016.

video on demand (VOD) Systems that allow users to watch video or hear audio when they choose, rather than at a specific time; content is delivered on a personal computer or interactive television system (smart TV).

video producer The top executive of an online video, television, or movie production; has ultimate responsibility for managing the project, including funding, budgeting, hiring, scheduling, and overseeing production.

viral Relating to a video, image, or piece of information that spreads very rapidly and widely across the internet; a video that goes viral may bring fame and money to its producer.

vlogging Making a video in which the host talks into a camera and the message is the most important aspect; a vlog might be a tutorial, product or movie review, or personal story.

YouTube channel The home page for a YouTube account, showing the account name, account type, list of videos uploaded, and user information uploaded by the account holder.

For More Information

Academy of Motion Picture Arts and Sciences (AMPAS)
8949 Wilshire Boulevard
Beverly Hills, CA 90211-1972
(310) 247-3000
Website: www.oscars.org

This is an honorary organization of motion-picture professionals
founded to advance the arts and sciences of motion
pictures.

Academy of Television Arts & Sciences
5220 Lankershim Boulevard
North Hollywood, CA 91601
(818) 754-2800
Website: www.emmys.tv

This is a nonprofit trade organization for the advancement of
telecommunication arts and sciences.

Black Filmmaker Foundation (BFF)
131 Varick Street, Suite 937
New York, NY 10013
(212) 253-1690
Website: www.castandcrewofcolor.org

This is a nonprofit organization supporting an online community
of people of color who work in film, TV, and new media.

Canadian Media Producers Association (CMPA)
601 Bank Street, 2nd floor
Ottawa, ON KIS 3T4

Canada
(613) 233-1444
Website: http://www.cmpa.ca/

CMPA is Canada's leading trade association for independent
media producers, representing more than 350 companies. It
includes a trainee program (the Screen-Based Media
Production Program) for Canadian applicants ages fifteen to
thirty.

Columbia College Hollywood
18618 Oxnard Street
Tarzana, California 91356-1411
(800) 785-0585
Website: http://www.columbiacollege.edu/academics/
degree-programs-study

This is one example of a college with a strong degree program
in media arts, including video production. Website includes
descriptions of degree programs, courses, core curriculum,
and summer programs for high school students.

Film Independent
9911 West Pico Boulevard, 11th floor
Los Angeles, CA 90035
(310) 432-1200
Website: www.filmindependent.org

This nonprofit arts organization supports independent films and
the artists who create them. It sponsors the Independent
Spirit Awards and Los Angeles Film Festival.

Hispanic Organization of Latin Actors (HOLA)
107 Suffolk Street, Suite 302
New York, NY 10002
(212) 253-1015

Website: www.hellohola.org

This service organization is committed to projecting Hispanic artists and culture into the mainstream of Anglo-American industry and culture.

OneMarketMedia (OMM)
Suite 100
523 Buchanan Crescent
Ottawa, ON K1J 7V2
Canada
(613) 747-8989
Website: http://onemarketmedia.com/

This Canadian video marketing agency is based in Ottawa and Toronto. The website describes how video production is being used to market products, including examples of videos.

Open Media Foundation
700 Kalamath Street
Denver, Colorado 80204
(720) 222-0159
Website: http://openmediafoundation.org/services/
video-production

This nonprofit video production organization produces videos for other nonprofits. The website includes many examples.

Producers Guild of America (PGA)
8530 Wilshire Boulevard, Suite 400
Beverly Hills, CA 90211
(310) 358-9020
Website: www.producersguild.org

PGA is an organization representing the interests of all members of the producing team.

Sundance Institute
1835 Three Kings Drive
Park City, Utah 84060
(435) 658-3456
Website: www.sundance.org/

This nonprofit organization was founded by Robert Redford to advance the work of filmmakers and storytellers. Sundance sponsors workshops for makers of feature films and documentaries; it also sponsors the Sundance Film Festival to honor the best independent filmmakers.

Women in Film (WIF)
6100 Wilshire Boulevard, Suite 710
Los Angeles, CA 90048
(323) 935-2211
Website: www.wif.org

This nonprofit organization is dedicated to helping women achieve their highest potential within the global entertainment, communications, and media industries and to preserving the legacy of women within those industries.

WEBSITES

Because of the changing nature of internet links, Rosen Publishing has developed an online list of websites related to the subject of this book. This site is updated regularly. Please use this link to access the list:

http://www.rosenlinks.com/TTHIC/video

For Further Reading

Alan, Randy. *How to Become a Production Assistant in Hollywood: Actionable Steps and Advice to Land the Job.* Kindle Edition, Amazon Digital Services LLC, 2016.

Ascher, Steven, and Edward Pincus. *The Filmmaker's Handbook: A Comprehensive Guide for the Digital Age,* 2013 ed. New York, NY: Plume, 2012.

Bartsch, Jeff. *Edit Better: Hollywood-Tested Strategies for Powerful Video Editing.* Kindle Edition, Amazon Digital Services LLC, 2014.

Blofield, Robert. *How to Make a Movie in 10 Easy Lessons: Learn How to Write, Direct, and Edit Your Own Film Without a Hollywood Budget.* Lake Forest, CA: Walter Foster Jr., 2015.

Chapman, C. C., and Mark Yoshimoto Nemcoff. *101 Steps to Making Videos Like a Pro.* Kindle Edition. Amazon Digital Services LLC, 2014.

Ciampa, Rob, and Theresa Moore. *YouTube Channels for Dummies,* 1st ed. Hoboken, NJ: For Dummies, 2015.

Erickson, Gunnar, Mark Halloran, and Harris Tulchin. *Independent Film Producer's Survival Guide: A Business and Legal Sourcebook, 3rd ed.* New York, NY: Schirmer Trade Books, 2010.

Film School Online! *Filmmaking 101: Ten Essential Lessons for the Noob Filmmaker.* Kindle Edition, Amazon Digital Services LLC, 2012.

Goldman, John. *Filmmaking 101: How to Make a Movie.* Kindle Edition, Amazon Digital Services LLC, 2015.

Lancaster, Kurt. *Production House Cinema: Starting and Running Your Own Cinematic Storytelling Business.* New York, NY: Focal Press, Taylor & Francis Group, 2016.

Lanier, Troy, and Clay Nichols. *Filmmaking for Teens: Pulling Off Your Shorts,* 2nd ed. Studio City, CA: Michael Wiese Productions, 2010.

Lyons, Suzanne. *Indie Film Producing: The Craft of Low-Budget Filmmaking,* 1st ed. New York, NY: Focal Press, Taylor & Francis Group, 2012.

Martell, Carey. *The Lean Channel: YouTube for Entrepreneurs.* Martell Books, Kindle Edition, Amazon Digital Services LLC, 2015.

Mckinnon, Andrew. *YouTube: Ultimate YouTube Guide to Building a Channel, Audience, and to Start Making Passive Income.* CreateSpace Independent Publishing Platform, 2015.

Miller, Joel. *How to Make a No Budget Movie. Albion Entertainment Inc.* Kindle Edition, Amazon Digital Services LLC, 2011.

Schenk, Sonja, and Ben Long. *The Digital Filmmaking Handbook,* 5th ed. Boston, MA: Cengage Learning PTR, 2014.

Stockman, Steve. *How to Shoot Video That Doesn't Suck: Advice to Make Any Amateur Look Like a Pro.* New York, NY: Workman Publishing Company, 2011.

Strassner, Bunnie. *Media Artists: Create the Business of Your Dreams.* Kindle Edition, Amazon Digital Services LLC, 2015.

Walsh, Nick. *YouTube Secrets: How to Make $1,000+ Per Month on YouTube.* Kindle Edition, Amazon Digital Services LLC, 2016.

Willoughby, Nick. *Digital Filmmaking for Kids for Dummies.* Hoboken, NJ: For Dummies, 2015.

Bibliography

Artis, Anthony Q. *The Shut Up and Shoot Freelance Video Guide: A Down & Dirty DV Production*, 1st ed. New York, NY: Focal Press (Routledge, Taylor & Francis Group): 2011.

BigFuture by The College Board. "Major: Film Production." 2016. Retrieved Feb. 25, 2016. https://bigfuture. collegeboard.org/majors/arts-visual-performing-film -production.

Brouwer, Bree. "This Is How YouTubers Make Money." EContent. Oct. 16, 2014. Retrieved Feb. 25, 2016. http:// www.econtentmag.com/Articles/Column/Screen-Time/ This-is-How-YouTubers-Make-Money-99852.htm.

CareerPlanner.com. "Producer. Job Description – Part I." 1997– 2016. Retrieved Mar. 13, 2016. http://job-descriptions. careerplanner.com/Producers.cfm.

CareerPlanner.com. "Producer. Job Description and Skills Required – Part III." 1997–2016. Retrieved Feb. 25, 2016. http://job-descriptions.careerplanner.com/Producers-3.cfm.

CreativeSkillSet. "Production Runner." 2016. Retrieved Apr. 15, 2016. http://creativeskillset.org/job_roles/1701_production _runner.

DePaso, Richard. "The Future of Video Production." Aardvark Video & Media Productions. Dec. 8, 2015. Retrieved Mar. 1, 2016. https://aardvarkvideolasvegas.com/2015/12/ the-future-of-video-production/.

Downs, Zach. "How to Land a Job at a Video Production Company." 12 Stars Media. June 18, 2014. Retrieved Apr. 20, 2016. http://12starsmedia.com/blog/land-job-video -production-company.

Fox, Jimm. "The Future of Video Production – Chaos, Specialization, & Real Reality." One Market Media. Mar. 16, 2015. Retrieved Mar. 1, 2016. http://onemarketmedia. com/2015/03/16/the-future-of-video-production-chaos -specialization-real-reality/.

Halder, Gemma. "Job profiles: Television/film/video producer." AGCAS and Graduate Prospects Ltd. Dec. 2014. Retrieved Apr. 14, 2016. https://www.prospects.ac.uk/job-profiles/ television-film-video-producer.

Harrell, L. Scott. "12 Ways to Make Money with Your Smartphone or Video Camera." *Video Entrepreneur* Magazine. 2015. Retrieved Feb. 25, 2016. http://vtrep.com/ make-money-with-your-video-camera/.

IMDb. "Felix Kjellberg. Biography." 1990-2016. Retrieved Mar. 12, 2016. http://www.imdb.com/name/nm5579304/ bio?ref_=nm_ov_bio_sm.

Lanier, Troy and Clay Nichols. *Filmmaking for Teens. Pulling Off Your Shorts.* 2nd Edition. Studio City, CA: Michael Wiese Productions. 2010.

Millis, Rob. "Forward! The Digital Future: Embracing the Web Producers." Hope for Film. Jan. 11, 2016. Retrieved Apr. 22, 2016. http://trulyfreefilm.hopeforfilm.com/2013/01/forward -the-digital-future-embracing-the-web-producers.html.

Porter, H. Wolfgang. "Starting a Production Company: What You Need to Know." *Videomaker Magazine.* Apr. 1, 2012. Retrieved Apr. 20, 2016. http://www.videomaker.com/article/ c7/15423-starting-a-production-company-what-you-need -to-know.

Reel Marketer. "The Top 15 Online Video Production Courses." Mar. 21, 2016. http://www.reelmarketer.com/top-online- video-production-courses-list/.

Trinklein, Prof. Michael. "Production 101." 2014. Retrieved Mar. 21, 2016. http://www.video101course.com/.

Index

ABOUT THE AUTHOR

Carol Hand has a PhD in zoology. She has taught college, worked for standardized testing companies, developed multimedia science and technology curricula, and written more than thirty science and technology books for young people. She loves going to movies, occasionally gets hooked on television series, and has absorbed a lot about film and video making since her son attended film school.

PHOTO CREDITS

Cover Stock image/Shutterstock.com; p. 5 © AP Images p. 7 Stock-Asso/Shutterstock.com; pp. 10–11 Aleksandr/ Shutterstock.com; p. 13 Debby Wong/Shutterstock.com; p. 17 Featureflash Photo Agency/Shutterstock.com; p. 19 AF archive/ Alamy Stock Photo; p. 21 Pavel Ilyukhin/Shutterstock.com; p. 23 Riccardo Mayer/Shutterstock.com; p. 26 Sean Pavone/ Shutterstock.com; p. 29 marco mayer/Shutterstock.com; p. 31 JuliusKielaitis/Shutterstock.com; p. 35 Rena Schild/Shutterstock .com; p. 36 Sergey Lavrentev/Shutterstock.com; p. 38 aquapix/ Shutterstock.com; p. 40 Pressmaster/Shutterstock.com; p. 42 © Bernd Tschakert Photography/Alamy Stock Photo; p. 44 racorn/Shutterstock.com; p. 47 © iStockphoto.com/Szepy; p. 51 Jeff Kravitz/FilmMagic/Getty Images; pp. 54–55 Bloomberg/ Getty Images; p. 57 John Shearer/Getty Images; p. 60 Monkey Business Images/Shutterstock.com; pp. 62–63 Jemal Countess/ Getty Images; back cover and interior pages background image Vladgrin/Shutterstock.com.

Designer: Nicole Russo; Editor: Bethany Bryan;
Photo Researcher: Bethany Bryan